HOW TO DRAW CUTE HEROES AND HEROINES

How To Draw Cute Heroes and Heroines

 Dawn MacDonald

Silver Dolphin

San Diego, California

Silver Dolphin Books
An imprint of Printers Row Publishing Group
A division of Readerlink Distribution Services, LLC
10350 Barnes Canyon Road, Suite 100, San Diego, CA 92121
www.silverdolphinbooks.com

Printers Row Publishing Group is a division of Readerlink
Distribution Services, LLC.
Silver Dolphin Books is a registered trademark of
Readerlink Distribution Services, LLC.

All notations of errors or omissions should be addressed
to Silver Dolphin Books, Editorial Department, at the
above address. All other correspondence (author
inquiries, permissions) concerning the content of
this book should be addressed to:
Quarto Publishing plc, 6 Blundell Street
London, N7 9BH, UK.
QUAR. 335795

ISBN: 978-1-64517-454-7
Manufactured, printed, and assembled in
Guangdong, China.
First printing, July 2020. TEN/07/20
24 23 22 21 20 1 2 3 4 5

CONTENTS

INTRODUCTION

Hello! My name is Dawn MacDonald, and I've been an avid artist since the tender age of six years old, when I discovered pencils and paper. The first things I loved to draw were cartoons and dragons, and as the years progressed, I developed a thirst for drawing anything and everything.

I was thrilled to be given the opportunity to draw some of the most prominent people in history for this guidebook, highlighting different icons from the worlds of art and music—subjects that have personally inspired and motivated me—to science and sports. By following the cute and easy *chibi* style, any young artist can advance their own drawing skills.

Each character is drawn in stages, starting with basic guides that plot the main shapes of the person's pose. Sketch these lightly, as you will draw your final artwork on top. Follow each step and the drawing will come together using outlines that can be colored when finished.

Discover pivotal figures who have influenced our world through art, activism, music, science, literature, and sports—amazing people from the past and those currently making a difference. Practice makes perfect, so follow the tutorials and take inspiration from the heroes and heroines you're about to bring to life!

ART
MATERIALS

THERE ARE SO MANY DIFFERENT TOOLS AVAILABLE THAT CAN BE USED TO DRAW AND COLOR CUTE HEROES AND HEROINES. THESE ARE SOME OF THE MATERIALS THAT I LOVE THE MOST.

PAPER
You don't need a specific kind of paper; any drawing surface is fine, but graph paper will help when plotting the guides. Use a sketchbook or notebook to keep all your drawings together. If you like to paint, use thicker paper, so it won't wrinkle as much.

PENS

These are my favorite tools! Pens are great when you want a thin stroke or a precise line. They are perfect for facial expressions and details. Try technical drawing pens to get a perfect line for borders and straight edges.

MARKERS

These have wide tips that leave thicker, permanent marks. Test them first, since they can't be erased. Some art markers are light and create beautiful thick, paintlike strokes, perfect for coloring in!

CRAYONS

For lots of coloring, crayons can be fun. You can create thin strokes by pressing lightly, or press harder for rich colors and thicker lines.

PENCILS

Graphite pencil leads are graded hard (#3 or H) or soft (#1 or B for black). Some artists prefer the H pencil because it makes a very slight, gray line, which is perfect for light guidelines, but the lead can scratch the paper if you press too hard.

Mechanical pencils are refillable and designed to take a variety of leads. The advantage of a mechanical pencil is that it is sharp all the time, so the lead widths give you the choice of how delicate you want the pencil point to be and how thick or thin the line.

Colored pencils are ideal for sketching and creating fun accessories and outfits. Choose between traditional wooden pencils or mechanical pencils.

WATERCOLORS

Available in a palette or a tube in a vast range of colors, high-quality artists' watercolors are usually worth the extra cost. A tray of watercolors is easily portable, or use tube colors for creating washes.

Whether you use paints, pencils, pens, or crayons, figure out what is the most comfortable tool for you. Experiment with different colors, textures, and line widths to see your cute heroes truly come to life!

BRUSHES

You might prefer to paint your cute heroes, rather than draw them, or you could draw first, then paint. You will need two types of brushes: a thin brush for drawing and one or more round brushes for applying color. It can be a bit awkward to draw with a brush, as you have less control than with a pen.

MAHATMA GANDHI

HARRIET TUBMAN

MALALA YOUSAFZAI

GRETA THUNBERG

MARTIN LUTHER KING JR.

ABRAHAM LINCOLN

BARACK OBAMA

JAZZ JENNINGS

MANAL AL-SHARIF

LEADERS AND ACTIVISTS

MARLEY DIAS

MAHATMA GANDHI

LET'S START DRAWING MAHATMA GANDHI—A REVOLUTIONARY LAWYER WHO LED THE INDIAN CAMPAIGN FOR INDEPENDENCE FROM BRITISH COLONIAL RULE. HE WAS A GREAT POLITICIAN WHO PRACTICED NONVIOLENCE AND BECAME KNOWN AS THE FATHER OF THE NATION, INSPIRING MILLIONS OF PEOPLE!

Start by drawing the basic guides that form Gandhi's body.

1

Draw his head shape and add his ears.

2

Next, draw his glasses and the frames.

3

4 Now draw his eyes, facial features, and hairline.

5 Sketch his upper body and clothes.

6 Now draw his lower body and sandaled feet.

Here's how your artwork should look once you've drawn everything. Great work!

HARRIET TUBMAN

BORN INTO SLAVERY IN THE 1820s, HARRIET TUBMAN ESCAPED AND BECAME AN AMERICAN ABOLITIONIST AND POLITICAL ACTIVIST. SHE HELPED RESCUE HUNDREDS OF ENSLAVED PEOPLE USING A NETWORK OF SAFE HOUSES, KNOWN AS THE UNDERGROUND RAILROAD. LET'S PAY TRIBUTE TO HER COURAGE AND DRAW HER!

Start by drawing the guidelines for her face and body.

1

Next, add her facial features.

2

Add her hair and face shape.

3

Now draw her upper body and her clasped hands.

4

Once that's done, work on Harriet's skirt.

5

Lastly, fill in the final touches, like her shoes and the detailing on her clothes.

6

Be proud of your finished piece and share your drawing!

MALALA YOUSAFZAI

LET'S DRAW MALALA, AN ACTIVIST FOR FEMALE EDUCATION AND THE YOUNGEST NOBEL PRIZE LAUREATE. HAVING SURVIVED AN ATTACK AFTER CONTINUOUSLY SPEAKING OUT ON BEHALF OF GIRLS SEEKING AN EDUCATION, SHE HAS BECOME AN INSPIRING SYMBOL FOR FIGHTING FOR ONE'S BELIEFS.

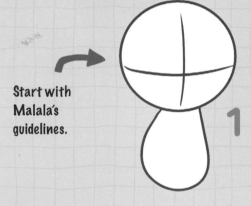

Start with Malala's guidelines.

1

Then, draw a larger circle outside the guides for her headscarf.

2

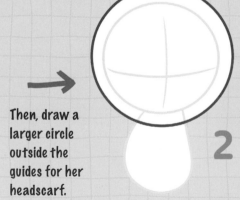

Next, draw a smaller circle inside the bigger one.

3

Now, draw her hair and facial features.

4

Time to draw the rest of her hijab and her hands.

5

Finally, draw the lower part of her body.

6

Now you can add some colors and patterns! Great job!

GRETA THUNBERG

GRETA THUNBERG WAS ONLY FIFTEEN WHEN SHE STARTED "SCHOOL STRIKE FOR CLIMATE" IN SWEDEN. HER CAUSE WAS SOON EMBRACED BY MILLIONS ALL OVER THE WORLD AND CALLS FOR POLITICAL LEADERS TO DO MORE TO PREVENT CLIMATE CHANGE. LET'S DRAW GRETA!

Begin by drawing the basic guides for Greta's pose.

1

Next, add her face shape, hair, and mouth.

2

Fill in her eyes and eyebrows, and her braids.

3

Now add a
beanie under
her hood.

4

Sketch in her
hood and then
her arms.

5

Finish by
drawing the rest
of her raincoat,
legs, and shoes.

6

Compare your
drawing—it should
look like this.
Excellent work,
keep it up!

MARTIN LUTHER KING JR.

IN HIS FAMOUS "I HAVE A DREAM" SPEECH, MARTIN LUTHER KING JR. CALLED FOR AN END TO RACIAL DISCRIMINATION. LET'S RE-CREATE THIS INSPIRING PASTOR AND PASSIONATE LEADER OF THE CIVIL RIGHTS MOVEMENT, CHIBI STYLE!

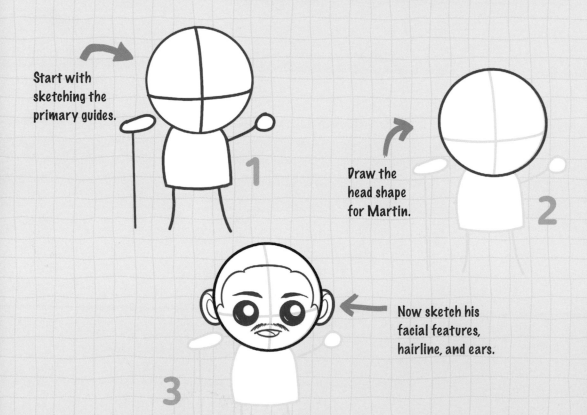

Start with sketching the primary guides.

1

Draw the head shape for Martin.

2

Now sketch his facial features, hairline, and ears.

3

Move on to
sketching his
torso and arms.

4

Draw the rest
of his suit,
shirt, and tie.

5

6

Then, draw his
pants and shoes.

7

Lastly, sketch a
microphone and
stand for him to
speak into.

Your final
drawing should
resemble this.
How easy was
that?

ABRAHAM LINCOLN

A STATESMAN AND HERO, "HONEST ABE" WAS THE 16TH PRESIDENT OF THE UNITED STATES. HE IS REMEMBERED FOR HIS MANY ACHIEVEMENTS, INCLUDING ABOLISHING SLAVERY, MODERNIZING THE U.S. ECONOMY, AND LEADING THE NATION THROUGH THE AMERICAN CIVIL WAR.

Begin by drawing the guidelines for Abe.

1

Next, draw the beginnings of his face.

2

Then, sketch in his facial features and the first stages of his hair.

3

Go ahead and
sketch his hat!

4

5

Then, draw
the left side
of his body.

6

Continue to draw
the right side of
his body.

7

Lastly, sketch his
legs and shoes.

Your final
sketch should
resemble this.
Very smart!

BARACK OBAMA

OBAMA WAS THE 44TH PRESIDENT OF THE UNITED STATES AND THE FIRST AFRICAN AMERICAN PRESIDENT IN U.S. HISTORY. HE WAS AN INSPIRATION FOR MANY PEOPLE—ESPECIALLY AMERICANS FROM DIFFERENT MINORITY ETHNIC GROUPS—DURING HIS TWO TERMS IN OFFICE. LET'S PAY TRIBUTE TO THIS NOBEL PEACE PRIZE WINNER!

Begin by drawing the primary guidelines for Obama.

Draw his face shape and ears, leaving a gap on the right ear for his flag overlay.

Next, draw his eyes, eyebrows, and mouth.

Now draw his hairline.

Next, add his raised right arm and a flag in his hand.

4

5

Sketch his left arm and then the rest of his body.

6

Lastly, finish drawing Obama's legs and shoes.

7

Take a moment to admire your drawing—you're becoming a pro!

JAZZ JENNINGS

HAVE SOME COLORS READY FOR WHEN YOU'VE FINISHED DRAWING YOUTUBE STAR AND LGBT ACTIVIST JAZZ JENNINGS. AS ONE OF THE YOUNGEST PUBLIC FIGURES TO BE IDENTIFIED AS TRANSGENDER, HER BRAVERY IS AN INSPIRATION FOR PEOPLE OF ANY AGE.

Begin drawing the guidelines for Jazz's body.

1

Then, draw her face and hairline.

2

Take your time to draw her long, pretty hair.

3

Finish her hair by drawing the flower headband.

Now it's time to draw her eyes and mouth.

4

5

Then, sketch her upper body with her interlocking hands.

6

7

Lastly, draw the rest of the upper and lower parts of her dress.

You've finished drawing Jazz! Time to add lots of color!

MANAL AL-SHARIF

FAMOUS FOR HER CAMPAIGN TO GIVE WOMEN THE RIGHT TO DRIVE IN SAUDI ARABIA, ACTIVIST AND COLUMNIST MANAL AL-SHARIF IS LIVING PROOF THAT ONE VOICE CAN MAKE A DIFFERENCE IN THE WORLD! READY TO DRAW HER?

Start by sketching her basic body guides.

1

Now draw her face shape and the edge of her headscarf.

2

Next, draw Manal's facial features—her mouth and eyes.

3

Now draw her headscarf, or hijab, that drapes below her neck.

4

Start to draw her upper body, arms, and hands—don't forget the microphone.

5

Work on drawing her lower body next and the microphone cord.

6

Finish by filling in the pattern for her headscarf.

7

All finished! Turn the page to learn about another person who's impacted our world.

MARLEY DIAS

SOCIAL ACTIVIST MARLEY DIAS'S INTERNATIONAL CAMPAIGN TO COLLECT AND DONATE BOOKS FEATURING AFRICAN AMERICAN GIRLS AS THE LEAD CHARACTER, #1000BLACKGIRLBOOKS, DREW ATTENTION TO THE LACK OF DIVERSITY IN CHILDREN'S LITERATURE. SHE STARTED HER MOVEMENT IN 2015, WHEN SHE WAS ONLY IN SIXTH GRADE.

Start with the simple guidelines to build her body.

1

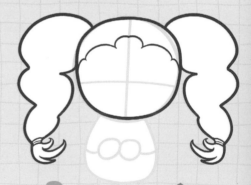

2

Then, draw Marley's head shape followed by her pigtails.

Sketch her eyes and then the glasses that frame them.

3

Now work on drawing her arms and the book she is holding.

4

Let's sketch her lower body and shoes!

5

6

Add shoelaces, and use thin lines to draw the pinstripes on her outfit—or leave it plain if you prefer.

Nicely done! Keep reading and drawing.

STEPHEN HAWKING

ALBERT EINSTEIN

MARIE CURIE

THOMAS EDISON

KATHERINE JOHNSON

ADA LOVELACE

NIKOLA TESLA

STEVE JOBS

ISAAC NEWTON

SACAGAWEA

AMELIA EARHART

THINKERS AND EXPLORERS

MAE JEMISON

NEIL ARMSTRONG

STEPHEN HAWKING

HERE'S A CHANCE TO DRAW THE BRILLIANT ENGLISH THEORETICAL PHYSICIST, COSMOLOGIST, AND AUTHOR STEPHEN HAWKING. DESPITE BEING DIAGNOSED WITH THE INCURABLE ILLNESS AMYOTROPHIC LATERAL SCLEROSIS (ALS) AT AGE 21, HAWKING LIVED FOR ANOTHER 55 YEARS AND WAS A PHENOMENAL SUCCESS, ATTRACTING HUGE CROWDS TO HIS LECTURES AND SELLING MILLIONS OF BOOKS.

Begin with the basic guidelines.

1

Then, draw his face shape and ears.

2

Next, sketch his hair and hairline.

3

Then, fill in the facial features and his eyeglass frames.

4

5

Now sketch his arms.

6

Draw his wheelchair next.

7

Next, sketch his legs and shoes.

8

Then, draw the rest of his wheelchair.

Show off your final line art and think about adding some color!

ALBERT EINSTEIN

NOW, HERE'S HOW TO DRAW ALBERT EINSTEIN. HE WAS A THEORETICAL PHYSICIST AND ONE OF THE GREATEST SCIENTIFIC MINDS OF ALL TIME. HE IS BEST KNOWN FOR DEVELOPING THE THEORY OF RELATIVITY AND THE EQUATION $E=MC^2$.

Begin by drawing the guides for Einstein.

1

Then, draw the simple face shape.

2

Now work on the hair shape for Einstein.

3

4

Next, draw his eyes and other facial features.

Now draw his body. Begin with the outer shape.

5

Finish with his feet, clothes, and the hand holding his pointer.

6

You've finished drawing Einstein! Now you're a genius, too!

MARIE CURIE

LET'S DRAW THE FIRST WOMAN IN HISTORY TO WIN A NOBEL PRIZE! MARIE CURIE WAS A POLISH-FRENCH SCIENTIST AND A PHYSICIST WHO DISCOVERED RADIATION, LEADING TO BREAKTHROUGHS IN THE TREATMENT OF CANCER AND MANY OTHER SCIENTIFIC ADVANCES.

First, draw the guidelines to form her body.

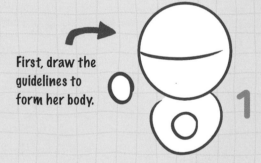

1

2

Next, draw Marie's face shape and ear.

3

Then, draw her eyes and other facial features.

4 Draw her hair and bun.

Start sketching her upper body and hands. **5**

Next, draw the test tubes she is holding, and then her dress. **6**

Once you're finished, she should look like this. Show off your drawing experiment!

THOMAS EDISON

HERE'S A CHANCE TO DRAW AMERICA'S GREATEST INVENTOR, THOMAS EDISON! HE INVENTED THE PHONOGRAPH, THE MOTION PICTURE CAMERA, AND THE ELECTRIC LIGHT BULB, ALL OF WHICH HAVE MADE SO MUCH POSSIBLE IN THE MODERN WORLD.

Let's begin sketching the body guidelines.

1

Now draw his face shape and his hair.

2

Time to add Thomas's facial features.

3

Then, draw his bowtie and collar of his shirt.

4

5

Move on to adding his arms and upper body.

Add his legs in a sitting position.

6

Go ahead and add his shoes.

7

8

Lastly, draw the chair he is sitting on as well as the light bulb in his hand.

Brilliant! Once everything has been drawn, pat yourself on the back—you've just drawn Thomas Edison!

KATHERINE JOHNSON

MATHEMATICIAN KATHERINE JOHNSON WAS ONE OF THE FIRST AFRICAN AMERICAN WOMEN TO WORK AS A NASA SCIENTIST. HER CALCULATIONS HELPED NASA LAUNCH ITS FIRST MANNED SPACEFLIGHTS IN THE 1960s. IT'S YOUR MISSION TO DRAW HER!

Begin with drawing her basic guidelines.

1

Now draw her face shape as well as her hairline and hair.

2

Next, sketch in her facial features.

3

Then, draw the cat-eye glasses that frame her eyes.

4

Now add her upper body, shirt collar, and NASA badge.

5

Finish the details of her upper body.

6

7

Give yourself a big thumbs-up, you've learned how to draw Katherine Johnson! Now add some color!

Now draw her skirt and high heels.

ADA LOVELACE

ADA LOVELACE WAS BORN IN 1815, THE DAUGHTER OF BRITISH POET LORD BYRON. THOUGHT TO HAVE BEEN THE FIRST COMPUTER PROGRAMMER, SHE WAS A MATHEMATICIAN WITH A BRILLIANT ANALYTICAL MIND. LET'S LEARN HOW TO DRAW HER IN SEVEN STEPS!

Begin with the simple guidelines for Ada's head and body.

1

Then, draw the head shape as well as her two hair buns.

2

Now fill in her facial features.

3

Next, draw her floral hairpiece.

4

Then draw her fancy collar.

5

Sketch her arm and then her dress.

6

7

Lastly, draw the flowery pattern on her dress.

All finished! If it seems like something is missing from the equation, add color to Ada's outfit.

NIKOLA TESLA

SERBIAN-AMERICAN INVENTOR NIKOLA TESLA IS BEST KNOWN FOR HIS DESIGN OF THE MODERN ALTERNATING CURRENT (AC) ELECTRICITY SUPPLY SYSTEM. FOR A BIT OF FUN, ADD A POWERFUL ELECTRICAL CURRENT ABOVE HIM, AS EVERYONE THOUGHT HE WAS A MAGICIAN IN HIS DAY!

Start with the guidelines for Nikola.

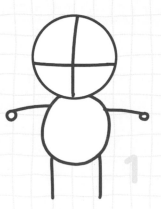

1

Then, draw his face shape, ears, and his hair.

2

Next, draw his facial features; don't forget to draw his mustache!

3

Sketch his upper body and hands. Start with his tie first.

Then, draw his legs and shoes.

Lastly, draw the electrical current above him.

What color is electricity? Add your own choice to the glowing current above Nikola!

STEVE JOBS

THE CO-FOUNDER AND FORMER CEO OF APPLE, STEVE JOBS WAS THE VISIONARY COMPUTER SCIENTIST RESPONSIBLE FOR THE iPHONE, iPOD, AND iPAD. HE WAS ALSO FAMOUS FOR HIS BASIC OUTFIT OF A BLACK TURTLENECK, BLUE JEANS, AND SNEAKERS, ALL OF WHICH WE'LL INCLUDE HERE—LET'S GET STARTED!

Begin with the simple guides to shape Steve's body.

1

Then, draw a circle shape for his head.

2

3

Next, draw his hairline and ears.

Now draw his
facial features
and glasses.

5

Sketch his upper
body and a phone
in his hand.

6

Then, finish off by
drawing his legs and
shoes. Don't forget
his other hand!

Here's the finished
drawing, ready
to be colored in.
Outstanding!

ISAAC NEWTON

GET YOUR PENCILS READY FOR ISAAC NEWTON!
BORN IN 1642, HE WAS A MATHEMATICIAN,
PHYSICIST, AND ASTRONOMER. HIS THEORY OF
GRAVITY CHANGED THE WORLD—HE OFTEN SAID HE
WAS INSPIRED TO FORMULATE HIS THEORY WHILE
WATCHING AN APPLE FALL FROM A TREE.

Start with the
simple guides
for Isaac.

1

Next, sketch the
shape of his face
and hairline.

2

Then, draw his
big curls of hair.

3

Now fill in his facial features.

Then, start sketching his upper torso and an apple in his hand.

Next, sketch his robe.

Finish by drawing the rest of the robe's details.

What color is the apple? Add some more details to bring Isaac to life!

SACAGAWEA

TIME TO DRAW SACAGAWEA, THE SHOSHONE WOMAN WHO TRAVELED THOUSANDS OF MILES WITH THE LEWIS AND CLARK EXPEDITION, FROM NORTH DAKOTA TO THE PACIFIC OCEAN. SHE HELPED THE EXPLORERS ESTABLISH CONTACT WITH DIFFERENT NATIVE AMERICAN POPULATIONS THROUGHOUT NORTH AMERICA. HER KNOWLEDGE OF THE NATURAL WORLD MADE HER ESSENTIAL TO THEIR TEAM.

Begin sketching her guidelines.

Then, move on to drawing her face shape and hairline.

Now sketch the facial features.

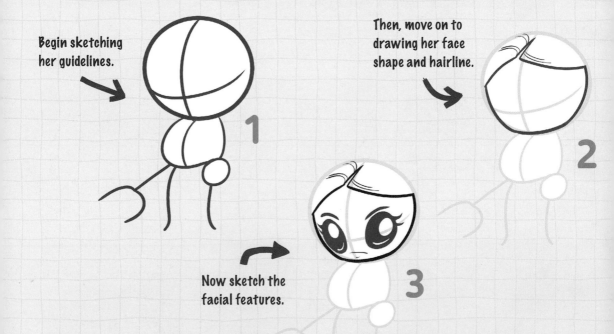

4

After, draw her hair in two pigtails.

Next, draw her ear and then her upper body.

5

Start sketching her dress and its details.

6

7

After, draw her moccasins. Take your time.

Lastly, finish by drawing her staff.

8

Now that you've completed drawing Sacagawea, turn the page for your next adventure in drawing!

AMELIA EARHART

IN 1932, AMELIA EARHART BECAME THE FIRST FEMALE PILOT TO FLY SOLO ACROSS THE ATLANTIC OCEAN, BECOMING A WORLDWIDE CELEBRITY AND INSPIRATION FOR OTHER ADVENTUROUS YOUNG PEOPLE. HER DISAPPEARANCE IN 1937, WHILE ATTEMPTING TO FLY AROUND THE GLOBE, CONTINUES TO REMAIN A MYSTERY. LET'S DRAW THIS FEARLESS PIONEER!

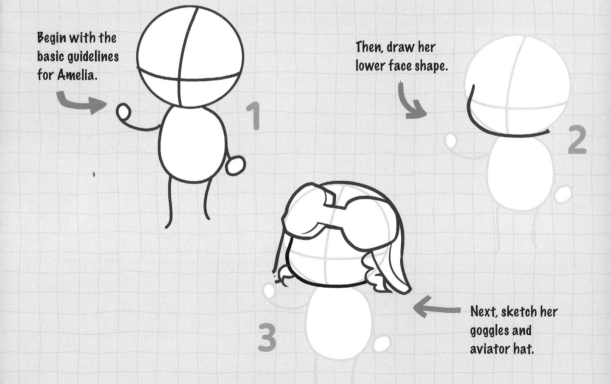

Begin with the basic guidelines for Amelia.

1

Then, draw her lower face shape.

2

Next, sketch her goggles and aviator hat.

3

Now draw her facial features.

Then, draw the interiors of the goggles.

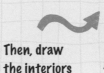

4

5

6

Let's work on her upper body and hands.

7

Lastly, sketch the lower body.

Add some color to your finished drawing, and you're ready for takeoff!

MAE JEMISON

GET YOUR PAPER AND PENCILS READY AND START THE COUNTDOWN TO DRAW MAE JEMISON, THE FIRST AFRICAN AMERICAN WOMAN TO TRAVEL INTO SPACE! A FORMER ASTRONAUT FOR NASA, SHE WAS A MISSION SPECIALIST ONBOARD THE SPACE SHUTTLE ENDEAVOUR IN 1992.

Begin by sketching the guides that will frame Mae's body and head.

1

Next, sketch her face, starting with the head shape.

2

Now draw her eyes and eyebrows.

3

Draw the ring for her space suit below her head.

Next, draw her upper body and hands holding her helmet.

Lastly, shade in the reflection on her helmet, then add her legs, and the emblems on her space suit.

Phew, that was hard work, but look what you've accomplished! Impressive!

☆ NEIL ARMSTRONG

SPACE FANS WILL LOVE THIS TUTORIAL OF NEIL ARMSTRONG, AN AMERICAN ASTRONAUT AND THE FIRST PERSON TO WALK ON THE MOON, MAKING HISTORY IN 1969. AS HE TOOK HIS FIRST STEPS, HE FAMOUSLY SAID: "THAT'S ONE SMALL STEP FOR [A] MAN, ONE GIANT LEAP FOR MANKIND."

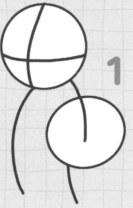

1

Let's draw the basic guidelines for Neil.

2

Then, sketch in his face shape and hairline, as well as his ear.

3

Next, draw the rest of his hair and details.

Sketch his torso, beginning with the arms.

Now draw the facial features for Neil.

4

5

Then, draw his neck and legs.

6

7

Now work on the rest of the space suit and his helmet!

When you're finished drawing, add some color to the flag and NASA badge. Great job!

DAVID BOWIE

AUDREY HEPBURN

BEYONCÉ

BRUCE LEE

SELENA

OPRAH WINFREY

CARMEN MIRANDA

MARILYN MONROE

ELVIS PRESLEY

ENTERTAINERS

DAVID BOWIE

VISIONARY, COLORFUL, AND FLAMBOYANT, DAVID BOWIE TRANSFORMED POP MUSIC IN THE '70s AND '80s. HERE'S A CHANCE TO DRAW ONE OF HIS MOST ICONIC LOOKS WITH A LIGHTNING BOLT PAINTED ACROSS HIS FACE, USED ON THE COVER OF HIS ALBUM *ALADDIN SANE*.

Begin by drawing the basic guides.

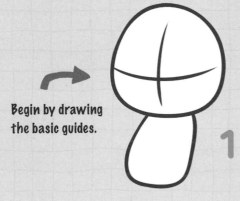

1

Then, draw Bowie's face shape and hairline.

2

Next, let's complete his hair.

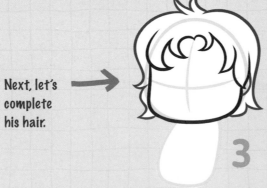

3

Draw in the
facial features
for Bowie.

4

Then, add the
lightning bolt
across his face.

5

Draw the
lapels of his
top—make
them wide!

6

Draw his legs
and torso.

7

8

Then, draw
his arms,
hands, and
boots.

Get Bowie ready
for the stage
by adding some
bright colors!

AUDREY HEPBURN

BELGIAN-BORN ACTOR, PHILANTHROPIST, AND FASHION ICON AUDREY HEPBURN IS CONSIDERED TO BE ONE OF THE MOST STYLISH AND ELEGANT SCREEN STARS IN CINEMATIC HISTORY. THE LOOK WE'RE GOING TO DRAW HERE IS INSPIRED BY HER MOST FAMOUS FILM ROLE—HOLLY GOLIGHTLY IN *BREAKFAST AT TIFFANY'S*.

Begin by drawing her body guidelines.

1

Then, draw her face shape and ear with an earring, as well as her bangs.

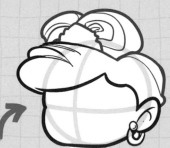

2

Next, draw her bun and back of her hairline.

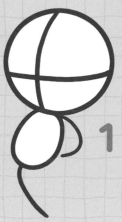

3

4

Next, draw Audrey's facial features.

5

Now draw her body, from top to bottom—don't forget to add a pearl necklace.

6

Then, finish by drawing a belt, the rest of her arm, and glove details.

She's ready for the red carpet! Shade her dress with elegant black.

BEYONCÉ

HAVING SOLD MORE THAN 100 MILLION ALBUMS, BEYONCÉ IS ONE OF THE MOST FAMOUS SINGERS AND DANCERS IN THE WORLD, AND HAS INFLUENCED A GENERATION OF YOUNG BLACK WOMEN. LET'S DRAW THE MULTITALENTED QUEEN B!

Draw the simple guide shapes.

1

Then, draw Bey's face shape.

2

Next, let's draw her facial features.

3

4

Now add a big bun with long hair below it.

Time to draw her body! Begin with her torso first.

5

Finish the body and then add Beyoncé's outfit and boots!

6

What a workout! Now add some color and sparkle to this amazing performer.

BRUCE LEE

NOW LET'S DRAW BRUCE LEE, ONE OF THE MOST ICONIC MARTIAL ARTISTS OF ALL TIME. WITH HIS POPULARITY AND INFLUENCE AS AN ACTOR AND DIRECTOR, HE HELPED TO CHANGE THE WAY ASIAN PEOPLE ARE REPRESENTED ON SCREEN. LET'S PAY TRIBUTE TO BRUCE LEE'S REMARKABLE CAREER WITH A DRAWING!

Build the guidelines for Bruce by sketching basic shapes for his body.

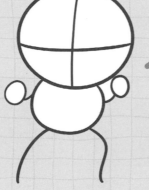

1

Then, add the hair shape to frame his head.

2

Next, draw his face and hairline.

3

Now sketch in his facial features.

4

5

Next, draw his fists and arms, ready for action!

6

Sketch in more of his upper and lower body.

7

Then, draw his belt and shoes.

Is your completed drawing ready for some kung fu fighting?

SELENA

WIDELY FOLLOWED AND CELEBRATED IN THE 1990s, SELENA QUINTANILLA-PÉREZ WAS AN INSPIRATIONAL MEXICAN-AMERICAN SINGER WHO WAS NAMED "QUEEN OF TEJANO MUSIC." SHE WAS ALSO FAMOUS FOR HER UNIQUE SENSE OF STYLE—LET'S TRY TO CAPTURE HER BOLD SPIRIT IN THIS DRAWING!

Begin by drawing the body guidelines for Selena.

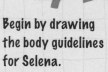

1

Next, work on the face shape, earrings, and her hair that frames her face.

2

Now draw the facial features.

3

Move on to her hands and arms.

4

Next, draw her clothing with her coat on top.

5

Draw the rest of her outfit and body, making sure you work your way down to her shoes.

6

Now that you've drawn Selena, add some color and detail to her outfit. Amazing!

OPRAH WINFREY

HAVE YOUR PENS AT THE READY TO DRAW THIS FABULOUS SUPERSTAR! OPRAH WINFREY IS BEST KNOWN FOR HER POPULAR TELEVISION TALK SHOW, WHICH RAN FOR TWENTY-FIVE YEARS. OPRAH IS ALSO BELOVED FOR HER GENEROSITY AND CHARITABLE CONTRIBUTIONS. SHE IS ONE OF THE MOST ICONIC AFRICAN AMERICAN WOMEN IN HISTORY, AND AMERICA'S FIRST BLACK MULTIBILLIONAIRE.

Start with the basic guides to draw Oprah.

1

Then, draw her classic cat-eye glasses.

2

3

Now sketch her facial features and eyes behind the glasses.

4

Next, draw her face shape.

Then, sketch her curly hair and earrings.

5

6

Sketch in her upper body and dress.

7

Lastly, draw her feet and legs.

Choose some vibrant, fun colors and color in your drawing!

CARMEN MIRANDA

THERE'S LOTS OF ACCESSORIES TO ADD TO FILM AND FASHION ICON CARMEN MIRANDA, WHO WAS NICKNAMED THE "BRAZILIAN BOMBSHELL" BACK IN THE 1940s. SHE WAS FAMOUS FOR HER SINGING, DANCING, AND UNFORGETTABLE FRUIT HAT. LET'S RE-CREATE THIS LIVELY SAMBA PERFORMER—AND HER FAMOUS HAT!

Begin with the basic guidelines for her figure.

1

Draw her face shape, hairline, and ears with big hoop earrings.

2

Next, draw her facial features!

3

4 Then, draw her famous fruit hat, with a little bit of hair showing underneath.

5 Next, sketch her upper body and her maracas.

6 Now sketch Carmen's dress and bottom ruffles.

7 Then, draw her legs and dress details.

There's plenty to color in once you've finished Carmen's spectacular outfit!

MARILYN MONROE

HOLLYWOOD'S SWEETHEART, INSTANTLY RECOGNIZABLE WITH HER PLATINUM BLOND HAIR AND RED LIPSTICK, MARILYN MONROE WAS A TALENTED ACTOR AND FASHION ICON. LET'S CELEBRATE HER IN THIS DRAWING INSPIRED BY A FAMOUS SCENE FROM *THE SEVEN YEAR ITCH*.

Start with the basic guidelines for Marilyn.

1

Then, draw the face shape and outline her hairline.

2

Next, draw her iconic hairstyle.

3

4

Now draw her facial features!

5

Then, draw her upper body and hands.

6

Sketch her dress that she is trying to push down.

7

Finish by sketching her legs and shoes.

Is your drawing ready for the walk of fame?

ELVIS PRESLEY

THE BEST-SELLING SOLO ARTIST IN THE HISTORY OF RECORDED MUSIC, ROCK 'N' ROLL MUSICIAN AND ACTOR ELVIS BECAME A GLOBAL ICON IN THE '50s AND '60s—EVENTUALLY, HE WAS NICKNAMED SIMPLY "THE KING." LET'S DRAW THIS LEGEND!

Begin by drawing the essential guidelines for Elvis.

1

Then, draw the King's face shape, as well as his hairline.

2

Next, draw his pompadour and sideburns.

3

Now let's sketch his facial features.

Next, draw his upper body, arm, and hand.

4

5

Now sketch his lower body and pants.

6

7

Lastly, finish the rest of his clothing and then add the microphone he is holding.

Your Elvis is ready for some "Jailhouse Rock"! Now add some color.

MISTY COPELAND

GET YOUR PENCILS READY TO DRAW AMERICAN BALLET DANCER MISTY COPELAND. SHE IS THE FIRST AFRICAN AMERICAN PRINCIPAL DANCER IN THE 75-YEAR HISTORY OF THE AMERICAN BALLET THEATRE. HER PERFORMANCES ARE EXTRAORDINARY TO WATCH AS SHE GRACEFULLY TAKES HOLD OF THE STAGE.

Start with the simple guidelines to shape her body and pose.

1

Then, sketch her face shape and hair.

2

3

Sketch her eyes and mouth.

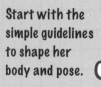

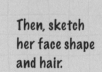

Let's start on her pose! Work down from her torso to her pointe shoes.

4

Fill in her arms and then start on her leotard. Finish Misty's hair.

5

6

Now add the rest of her beautiful flowing dress!

Once you're done, you should have something very similar to this. Brava!

FRIDA KAHLO

PABLO PICASSO

MARY SHELLEY

MAYA ANGELOU

WILLIAM SHAKESPEARE

J.K. ROWLING

VINCENT VAN GOGH

ANNA WINTOUR

ANDY WARHOL

LEONARDO DA VINCI

ANNE FRANK

ARTISTS AND WRITERS

EDGAR ALLAN POE

FRIDA KAHLO

TIME TO DRAW FRIDA KAHLO, ONE OF THE MOST FAMOUS ARTISTS OF THE TWENTIETH CENTURY. HER COLORFUL SELF-PORTRAITS, FEATURING FLOWERS, ANIMALS, AND FRUIT, WERE INSPIRED BY THE FOLK ART AND NATURAL SETTINGS OF HER NATIVE MEXICO.

Draw the basic guides for Frida's head and body.

1

Draw her face and simple hair shape.

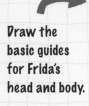

2

Add her distinct eyebrows, then her eyes, followed by the rest of her face.

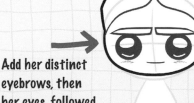

3

Next, draw ears and hoop earrings to frame her face.

4

Draw the collar
around her neck.

5

6

Then, draw her
left shoulder
and left arm.

Add her right
shoulder and
right arm.

7

Next, draw
the skirt of
her dress.

8

Lastly, draw
the flowers in
the center of
her head.

9

After everything
is drawn to your
liking, you can
start coloring
her in!

PABLO PICASSO

LET'S LEARN TO DRAW ONE OF THE MOST ORIGINAL ARTISTS IN HISTORY! PICASSO WAS A PROLIFIC SPANISH PAINTER AND SCULPTOR WHO CO-FOUNDED THE ABSTRACT STYLE OF CUBISM AND INFLUENCED THE DEVELOPMENT OF MODERN ART. HIS PAINTINGS HAVE SOLD FOR HUNDREDS OF MILLIONS OF DOLLARS.

Start off by drawing the simple guidelines.

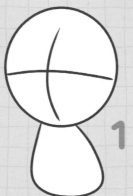

1

Then, draw Picasso's head shape.

2

3

Now draw the hair framing his face and the ear.

Next, draw Picasso's facial features— make sure you add wrinkles!

4

Now draw his arms raised, holding the paintbrush.

5

Draw the rest of his body and shoes.

6

Finish by drawing the iconic stripes on his shirt and finish the details of his pants.

7

Step back and admire your masterpiece!

MARY SHELLEY

ARE YOU READY TO DRAW NOVELIST MARY SHELLEY, AUTHOR OF *FRANKENSTEIN*? MARY WAS ONLY EIGHTEEN WHEN SHE STARTED THE STORY—THOUGHT TO BE THE FIRST WORK OF SCIENCE FICTION—ABOUT A SCIENTIST AND HIS FRIGHTENING CREATION. SHELLEY'S NOVEL CONTINUES TO BE HUGELY INFLUENTIAL IN POP CULTURE.

Draw Mary's head and body guidelines first.

1

Next, draw her head shape.

2

Move on to draw the hair that frames her head.

3

Now draw her
eyes and mouth.

4

Let's start
working on her
upper body and
draw her arms.

5

6

Using thin lines,
draw her collar
and waist.

7

Lastly, finish the
rest of her dress.

Look what
you created!
Fantastic!

MAYA ANGELOU

AN AFRICAN AMERICAN WRITER, POET, AND ACTOR, MAYA ANGELOU IS MOST FAMOUS FOR HER MEMOIR, *I KNOW WHY THE CAGED BIRD SINGS*. SHE WAS ALSO A CIVIL RIGHTS ACTIVIST WHO WORKED WITH MARTIN LUTHER KING JR. LET'S HONOR HER LEGACY WITH A DRAWING!

Draw the simple guidelines for the head and body.

1

Sketch Maya's head first, and then her facial features.

2

Now shade the insides of her eyes.

3

Work on drawing her head wrap next.

4

Sketch her torso, starting with her collar and then her arms.

5

Draw her hands and the dress.

6

Don't forget to draw her shoes!

7

Add color and pattern to Maya's outfit when your drawing is finished.

WILLIAM SHAKESPEARE

LET'S PUT PEN TO PAPER AND DRAW THE WORLD'S MOST FAMOUS PLAYWRIGHT, WILLIAM SHAKESPEARE! HIS PLAYS—WHICH INCLUDE *ROMEO AND JULIET*, *MACBETH*, *A MIDSUMMER NIGHT'S DREAM*, AND MANY OTHERS—ARE PERFORMED MORE OFTEN THAN THOSE OF ANY OTHER DRAMATIST IN THE WORLD.

1

First, draw the basic guidelines for his body.

2

Then, draw William's facial features, plus mustache and goatee.

3

Next, begin drawing his face shape and ear.

Now draw his wavy hair and earring.

4

Then, add his body, beginning with the ruff around his neck.

5

6

Next, draw the legs and vest.

Finish off by drawing his beard, the quill pen, and pants seam!

7

Your finished drawing should look like this. Applause!

J.K. ROWLING

LET'S CONJURE A GREAT DRAWING OF BRITISH AUTHOR J.K. ROWLING, WHO WROTE THE HARRY POTTER NOVELS, THE HIGHEST-SELLING BOOK SERIES IN HISTORY. SHE HAS MADE A HUGE IMPACT ON THE WORLD WITH HER MAGICAL IMAGINATION AND BELOVED CHARACTERS.

Begin by drawing the basic guidelines for her body and head.

1

Next, sketch her face shape as well as her hair to frame her forehead. Add earrings to her ears.

2

Then, draw her facial features.

3

Complete her head by finishing her hair.

4

Work on her body next, starting with her arms.

5

6

Then, add her necklaces and collar.

7

Next, draw her book!

8

Finish by drawing her legs and shoes!

Once you're all done, your drawing will look like this. Magic!

VINCENT VAN GOGH

LET'S PAY TRIBUTE TO THE AMAZING TALENT OF POST-IMPRESSIONIST PAINTER VINCENT VAN GOGH, ONE OF THE MOST VISIONARY ARTISTS IN HISTORY. HE WAS FAMOUS FOR HIS EXPRESSIVE BRUSHSTROKES AND VIBRANT USE OF COLOR. VAN GOGH CREATED OVER 2,000 WORKS OF ART IN HIS LIFETIME.

First, draw the body guidelines for Vincent's pose.

1

Now draw the lower part of his face, his beard, and ear.

2

Next, add the hair to frame his face and head shape.

3

Then draw his facial features.

4

Sketch in the upper body, with one hand holding a paintbrush and the other holding a canvas.

5

Finish by drawing his legs and shoes.

6

Take a bow— you've just drawn Vincent van Gogh!

ANNA WINTOUR

THE ONE AND ONLY ANNA WINTOUR HAS BEEN THE EDITOR-IN-CHIEF OF THE AMERICAN EDITION OF *VOGUE* SINCE 1988. HER ORIGINAL STYLE AND GENEROUS SUPPORT FOR YOUNG DESIGNERS HAS INFLUENCED THE FASHION INDUSTRY AROUND THE WORLD.

Draw guidelines for Anna's head and body.

1

Let's start with her bangs and her iconic hairstyle.

2

Now add her chin, mouth, and sunglasses.

3

Then, draw her necklace and fluffy wrap.

4

5

Lastly, draw her dress and the pattern details.

When finished, your drawing will be front-cover ready!

ANDY WARHOL

IN THIS TUTORIAL YOU'RE GOING TO DRAW ANDY WARHOL, AN ICONIC POP ARTIST WHO DEFINED THE 1960s. WARHOL'S MOST FAMOUS WORKS ARE SCREEN PRINTS OF CAMPBELL'S SOUP CANS AND CELEBRITIES SUCH AS MARILYN MONROE.

Let's start by drawing the face and body guides for Andy.

1

Next, draw his face shape and eyes.

2

Then, draw his glasses, mouth, and eyebrows.

3

Now draw his iconic platinum hair.

4

Next, draw the torso and hands holding his camera.

5

Lastly, sketch his lower body and shoes.

6

Your end result should look like this. Great practice!

LEONARDO DA VINCI

GET YOUR PENCILS READY TO DRAW ONE OF THE MOST LEGENDARY PAINTERS AND INVENTORS OF THE ITALIAN RENAISSANCE, LEONARDO DA VINCI. HIS MOST FAMOUS PAINTING IS THE *MONA LISA*, WHICH HANGS IN THE LOUVRE MUSEUM IN PARIS AND IS SEEN BY ABOUT 30,000 VISITORS EACH DAY.

Start with the simple guidelines for Leonardo.

1

Next, draw his hat and hair that frame his face.

2

Now draw his long beard.

3

4

Complete his head by drawing his facial features.

Draw the right side of his body, with his hand holding the paint palette.

5

Then, draw the left side of his body, adding a paintbrush in his hand.

6

7

Finish by drawing his lower body.

Voilà! Now you're a legend.

ANNE FRANK

ANNE FRANK WAS ONLY THIRTEEN YEARS OLD WHEN SHE AND HER FAMILY HAD TO GO INTO HIDING FROM THE NAZIS DURING WORLD WAR II. HER FAMOUS DIARY DESCRIBING HER EXPERIENCE OF BEING A JEWISH PERSON DURING THAT TIME HAS AFFECTED MILLIONS OF PEOPLE AROUND THE GLOBE. LET'S DRAW HER.

 Begin by drawing the guides for Anne's pose.

1

Then, draw her hair and face shape.

2

Keep working on her hair so that it frames her face shape!

3

5

Now sketch the collar of her shirt and her pendants.

Next, work on her facial features.

4

Then, draw her dress, legs, and shoes.

6

Lastly, draw the journal and pen in her hands.

7

This is what your finished drawing should look like. Well done!

EDGAR ALLAN POE

NINETEENTH-CENTURY AMERICAN WRITER EDGAR ALLAN POE WAS FAMOUS FOR HIS DARK AND MYSTERIOUS POEMS AND SHORT STORIES. WE WILL BE DRAWING HIM WITH A RAVEN FRIEND, "NEVERMORE," INSPIRED BY HIS MOST FAMOUS POEM, "THE RAVEN."

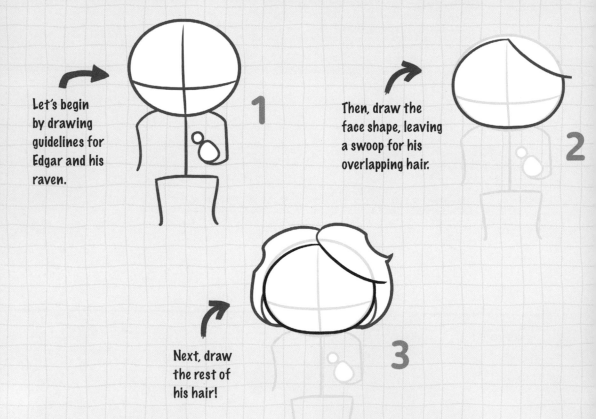

Let's begin by drawing guidelines for Edgar and his raven.

1

Then, draw the face shape, leaving a swoop for his overlapping hair.

2

Next, draw the rest of his hair!

3

Now draw his facial features and mustache.

4

Once that's done, sketch his upper body and raven.

5

6

Then, draw his suit and lower body.

7

Finish by drawing his pant creases and shoes.

This is what you should finish up with. Excellent work!

MUHAMMAD ALI

SERENA WILLIAMS

USAIN BOLT

SIMONE BILES

MEGAN RAPINOE

MICHAEL JORDAN

BABE RUTH

MICHELLE KWAN

SPORTS FIGURES

MUHAMMAD ALI

"FLOAT LIKE A BUTTERFLY, STING LIKE A BEE" IS A FAMOUS QUOTE FROM OLYMPIC GOLD MEDALIST MUHAMMAD ALI. HE CALLED HIMSELF "THE GREATEST" AFTER WINNING DOZENS OF HEAVYWEIGHT BOXING TITLES—ALI IS ONE OF THE MOST CELEBRATED ATHLETES OF ALL TIME.

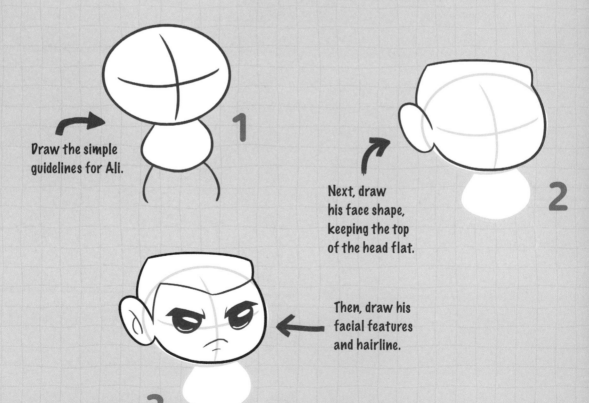

Draw the simple guidelines for Ali.

1

Next, draw his face shape, keeping the top of the head flat.

2

Then, draw his facial features and hairline.

3

Fill in his hair with black, leaving a thin line for the highlight.

4

Draw boxing gloves on each side of his body.

5

Now sketch his shorts.

6

7

Finish drawing him by adding his legs and shoes!

For the next round you can add color and shadows to your heavyweight champion!

SERENA WILLIAMS

TENNIS SUPERSTAR SERENA WILLIAMS HAS WON TWENTY-THREE GRAND SLAM SINGLES TITLES. ARE YOU READY TO DRAW THIS TRAILBLAZING ATHLETE WHO HAS INSPIRED A WHOLE NEW GENERATION OF TENNIS PLAYERS?

Begin by drawing the basic guidelines for Serena.

1

Then, draw her head shape and headband.

2

Next, draw her hair and hairline.

3

4

Now, draw her facial features as well.

5

Next, sketch her arm and hands that will be holding the tennis racket.

Then, draw her racket.

6

Let's add the strings to her racket and draw the grip as well.

7

8

Lastly, draw the tennis ball and her lower body.

Congrats! You've finished drawing Serena!

USAIN BOLT

HOLDER OF WORLD RECORDS FOR THE 100M, 200M, AND THE 4 X 100M RELAY, JAMAICAN ATHLETE USAIN BOLT IS CONSIDERED TO BE THE GREATEST SPRINTER OF ALL TIME AND THE FASTEST MAN ALIVE. HE IS WELL KNOWN FOR HIS FAMOUS STANCE—LET'S DRAW THIS LIGHTNING-FAST OLYMPIC GOLD MEDALIST!

Begin by drawing the guidelines for Usain.

1

2

Now sketch his head shape.

3

Next, draw his hairline, eyes, ear, and mouth.

Then, draw his raised arms in the "lightning bolt" pose!

4

Let's draw his outfit and lower body.

5

Don't forget to draw the lightning bolts on his shirt!

6

Your finished drawing should look like this. Nice job crossing the finish line!

SIMONE BILES

SOAR TO NEW HEIGHTS BY CAPTURING THE POWER AND GRACE OF ONE OF THE TOP GYMNASTS IN THE WORLD, SIMONE BILES. SHE IS THE MOST DECORATED AMERICAN GYMNAST IN HISTORY, WITH DOZENS OF MEDALS TO HER NAME.

Begin by drawing Simone's body guidelines—you can already see her dynamic pose.

1

Move on to drawing her face shape, as well as her ponytail flowing upward.

2

3

Next, draw her facial features and shade in the dark tone of her hair.

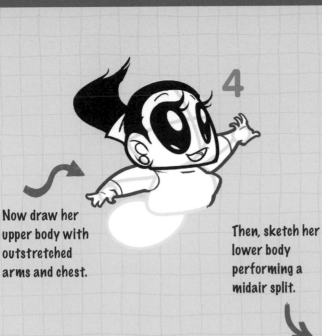

4

Now draw her upper body with outstretched arms and chest.

Then, sketch her lower body performing a midair split.

5

6

Lastly, add the medal around her neck!

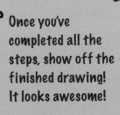

Once you've completed all the steps, show off the finished drawing! It looks awesome!

MEGAN RAPINOE

MEGAN RAPINOE PLAYS FOR THE NATIONAL WOMEN'S SOCCER LEAGUE AND CO-CAPTAINS THE UNITED STATES NATIONAL TEAM. HER DEDICATION AND POSITIVE LEADERSHIP HELPED HER TEAM WIN THE WORLD CUP IN 2019. SHE IS ALSO AN OUTSPOKEN ADVOCATE IN THE FIGHT FOR EQUAL PAY FOR WOMEN AND LGBT+ CAUSES.

Lightly draw the guidelines for Megan's body and head.

1

Draw Megan's face shape first and then her facial features.

2

Then, draw her swept-back hair.

3

Then, draw the rest of her shirt and lower body.

4

Sketch her left arm and collar.

5

6

Fill in her right arm, as well as her team emblems.

7

Finish by drawing a circle for the soccer ball and filling in the pattern.

You've got skills—keep practicing!

MICHAEL JORDAN

LET'S JUMP TO IT AND DRAW MJ, THE ALL-TIME GREATEST PROFESSIONAL BASKETBALL PLAYER. NICKNAMED "AIR JORDAN" FOR GRAVITY-DEFYING JUMPING ABILITY, HE PLAYED FIFTEEN SEASONS IN THE NBA, WINNING SIX CHAMPIONSHIP RINGS WITH THE CHICAGO BULLS.

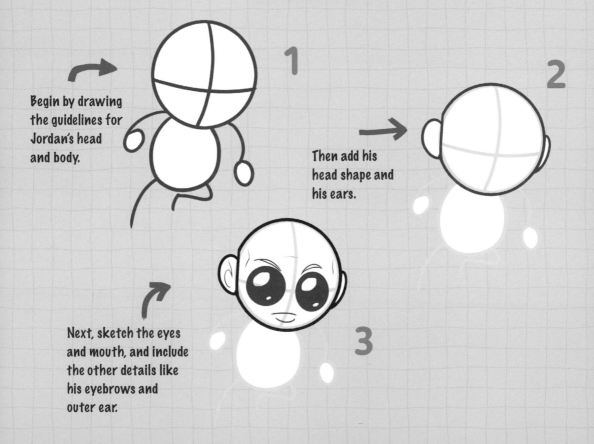

Begin by drawing the guidelines for Jordan's head and body.

1

Then add his head shape and his ears.

2

Next, sketch the eyes and mouth, and include the other details like his eyebrows and outer ear.

3

Then, draw his arms.

4

Draw his torso next.

5

Now add a basketball underneath his hand.

6

7

Draw his lower body and shorts.

8

Lastly, fill in his legs and shoes.

What a slam dunk! Now you can add some team colors!

BABE RUTH

LEGENDARY BASEBALL SUPERSTAR BABE RUTH PLAYED IN TWENTY-TWO MAJOR LEAGUE BASEBALL SEASONS, FIRST FOR THE BOSTON RED SOX, THEN THE NEW YORK YANKEES. HE SET A NUMBER OF BASEBALL RECORDS—SOME OF WHICH STILL HAVEN'T BEEN BEATEN. LET'S DRAW "THE GREAT BAMBINO"!

Start by sketching the body guidelines for Babe Ruth.

1

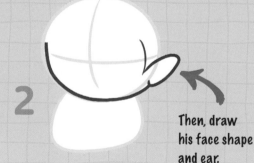

2

Then, draw his face shape and ear.

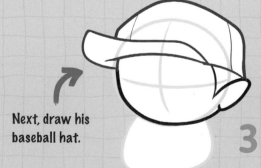

3

Next, draw his baseball hat.

Now sketch in his facial features and ear detailing.

4

Then add his upper body as well.

5

6

Now sketch the lower body, adding his belt.

7

Lastly, draw the baseball, bat, stripes on his uniform, and his shoes.

Time to share your drawing with admiring fans. You knocked it out of the park— home run!

MICHELLE KWAN

LET'S CELEBRATE THE REMARKABLE GRACE AND TALENT OF FIGURE SKATER MICHELLE KWAN. WITH DETERMINATION AND GRIT, SHE WON TWO OLYMPIC MEDALS AND MORE THAN FORTY U.S. AND WORLD CHAMPIONSHIPS.

Start with the guides to shape Michelle's body.

1

Then, draw her face shape.

2

Now frame her face with her hair in a bun.

3

Now sketch her facial features.

Next, draw the top part of her costume.

4

5

Now draw her legs! Start from the waist and work down to the ice skates.

6

7

Lastly, draw her outstretched arms!

Wow, you've successfully drawn Michelle Kwan. Stay focused and continue practicing!